The boy lifted his hand toward the smiling children;
then the animal hurried away with him
out through the open vestibule.

HANS CHRISTIAN ANDERSEN

*"Mark this:
Unless you accept God's kingdom
in the simplicity of a child,
you'll never get in."*

THE MESSAGE

LITERARY PORTALS TO PRAYER™

HANS CHRISTIAN ANDERSEN

ILLUMINATED BY

COMPILED AND INTRODUCED BY

MARY K. DOYLE

*To Carol,
May we trust in
the Lord, like children.
Love,
Mary*

HANS CHRISTIAN ANDERSEN
Illuminated by *The Message*
Compiled and introduced by Mary K. Doyle

Series Editor, Gregory F. Augustine Pierce
Design and typesetting by Harvest Graphics
Cover image © Irina Yun, under license from Bigstock

Published by ACTA Publications, 4848 N. Clark St.,
Chicago, IL 60640, (800) 397-2282, actapublications.com

Introduction and compilation copyright © 2015 by Mary K. Doyle

Scripture taken from *The Message: Catholic/Ecumenical Edition* Copyright © 2013 by
Eugene H. Petersen all rights reserved. Licensed with permission of NavPress. Represented
by Tyndale House Publishers Inc., Carol Stream, Illinois 60188.

The Message and *The Message* logo are registered trademarks of NavPress. Used by
permission. All rights reserved.

All rights reserved. No part of this publication may be reproduced or transmitted in any
form or by any means, electronic, digital, or mechanical, including photocopying and record-
ing, or by any information storage and retrieval system, including the Internet, without
permission from the publisher. Permission is hereby given to use short excerpts with proper
citation in reviews and marketing copy, newsletters, bulletins, class handouts, and scholarly
papers.

Library of Congress Number: 2015948514
ISBN: 978-0-87946-629-9 (standard edition)
ISBN: 978-0-87946-630-5 (enhanced-size edition)
Printed in the United States of America by Total Printing Systems
Year 20 19 18 17 16 15
Printing 12 11 10 9 8 7 6 5 4 3 2 First

♻ Text printed on 30% post-consumer recycled paper

CONTENTS

A NOTE FROM THE PUBLISHER / 9

INTRODUCTION / 11

PORTALS TO PRAYER / 13

FIRST AID 14
GREATER GIFTS,
    GREATER RESPONSIBILITIES 16
THE GIFT OF A HANDICAP 18
SALVATION BELONGS TO GOD 20
A PLAN TO CONTAIN THEM 22
YOUR RIGHTEOUSNESS
    IS ON EVERYONE'S LIPS 24
CONFIDENT IN YOUR VERDICT 26
THEY ABUSE ME 28
BE A BLESSING AND GET A BLESSING 30
PURITY OF HEART 32
MONEY DECEIVES 34
LET'S RUN OFF TOGETHER 36
LEAVE YOUR COUNTRY 38
LOVE FOREVER 40
STRIKE UP THE BAND 42
DIVERSITY OF RESURRECTION GLORY 44
TALKING NONSENSE,
    NOISY NONSENSE 46
A RIGHT TIME FOR BIRTH
    AND ANOTHER FOR DEATH 48
PROUD AND ARROGANT 50
A TRUE WITNESS NEVER LIES 52
YOU'LL ONLY LOOK FOOLISH YOURSELF .. 54
A GREAT PRETENSE OF SEEING 56
TWISTING THE TRUTH 58
BE WARY OF FALSE PREACHERS 60

A WILDLY WONDERFUL WORLD 62

SOME UNSUSPECTING SOUL 64

ANGELS TO GUARD YOU

      WHEREVER YOU GO 66

BABBLE 68

LAVISH GIFTS ON THE POOR 70

KEEP US SAFE 72

LIKE CHILDREN 74

FANTASY STORIES

      AND FANCIFUL FAMILY TREES 76

PRETENTIOUS EGOS

      BROUGHT DOWN TO EARTH 78

YOUR FUTURE IN HEAVEN 80

HE JUMPED TO HIS FEET AND WALKED ... 82

DRY BONES 84

SING FOR JOY 86

DON'T FALL FOR IT 88

A TIME OF RECKONING 90

AN ARROGANT CYNIC 92

BE COURTEOUSLY REVERENT

      TO ONE ANOTHER 94

NOT A WORD OF BOASTING 96

DON'T LET ME FALL

      INTO BAD COMPANY 98

ENJOY THE WIFE YOU MARRIED 100

TRUSTING IN OUR OWN STRENGTH 102

A NEW HEART 104

SEIZE LIFE! 106

BELIEVE IN THE LIGHT 108

THE KINGDOM'S PRIDE AND JOY 110

LET RIGHTEOUSNESS BURST

      INTO BLOSSOM 112

SCRIPTURE INDEX / 115

ABOUT MARY K. DOYLE / 117

IN MEMORY OF

my mother, Patricia M. Doyle,
and all those who read stories
of faith and promise to our world's children.

She had, however, almost reached the end of her labors; only one shirt of mail was wanting. But again she had no more flax and not a single nettle. Once more, for the last time, she must go to the churchyard to pluck a few handfuls. She thought with dread of the solitary walk and the horrible ghouls; but her will was as strong as her trust in God.

THE WILD SWANS

A NOTE FROM THE PUBLISHER

Prayer is sometimes difficult. Perhaps we need spiritual inspiration. Something to reignite our spiritual life. A way to initiate a new and fruitful spiritual direction.

Great literature can do these things: inspire, ignite, and initiate.

Which is why ACTA Publications is publishing a series of "Literary Portals to Prayer." The idea is simple: take insightful passages from great authors whose work has stood the test of time and illuminate each selection with a well-chosen quotation from the Bible on the same theme.

To do this, we use a relatively new translation by Eugene Peterson called *The Message: Catholic/Ecumenical Edition*. It is a fresh, compelling, challenging, and faith-filled translation of the Scriptures from ancient languages into contemporary American English that sounds as if it was written yesterday. *The Message* may be new to you, or you may already know it well, but see if it doesn't illuminate these writings of Hans Christian Andersen in delightful ways.

We publish the books in this series in a size that can easily fit in pocket or purse and find a spot on kitchen table, bed stand, work bench, study desk, or exercise machine. We also publish each title in an enhanced-size for both public and private use. These books are meant to be used in a variety of ways. And we feature a variety of authors so you can find the one or ones that can kick-start your prayer life.

So enjoy these portals to prayer by Hans Christian

Andersen illuminated by *The Message*. And look for others in this series, including Louisa May Alcott, Jane Austen, Charles Dickens, Elizabeth Gaskell, William Shakespeare, Herman Melville, and others. Consider them, if you will, literary lectio divina.

Gregory F. Augustine Pierce
President and Publisher
ACTA Publications

INTRODUCTION

The tiny and compassionate Thumbelina. The arrogant and proud Emperor and His New Clothes. The loneliness and humility of The Ugly Duckling.

My mother read these stories to me when I was a child from her own childhood book, titled *Andersen's Fairy Tales*. Curled up in her arms, I drifted off into the worlds created by Hans Christian Andersen. I heard the song of the Nightingale, cheered for Elise to complete the shirts necessary to change The Wild Swans back into her brothers, and longed to help Gerda find little Kay in The Snow Queen. I admired the courage of the imperfect Steadfast Tin Soldier and his love for the paper lady dancer in her cardboard castle.

Make-believe came to life with characters I could see and hear. Their problems were real to me. Their fears and joys were mine. Hans Christian Andersen created stories my mother and her children, as well as children of all ages, could relate to, and continue to do so for more than a century. Read around the world, these stories have been translated into more than 125 languages.

Although best known for his children's tales, Andersen (1805-1875) was also a playwright, novelist, poet, travel writer and illustrator, singer, and actor. Many believe that he was an illegitimate son of King Christian VIII of Denmark; however, he was raised in poverty by the father he knew and his mother, an uneducated washwoman. At an early age he was sent to live with an abusive schoolmaster.

His passion for writing was discouraged by his teachers. It wasn't until several of his works became successful that his confidence grew. One of his greatest joys was meeting Charles Dickens and then visiting his family in their home ten years later. Unfortunately, Dickens ended the friendship after Andersen overstayed his welcome, turning a short visit into five weeks. Andersen never understood why Dickens no longer responded to his letters.

Andersen's awkward search for love and friendship in his own life comes across in many of his tales. The underlying lessons and morals intertwined in his enchanting stories teach about loving one another, right and wrong, and the consequences of bullying, lying, and cheating. And many of his characters pray and call on God in their times of need.

Scripture easily compliments such themes. The 1936 edition of my mother's well-loved and well-worn *Andersen's Fairy Tales* disintegrated in my hands as I re-read and copied passages from it for this Literary Portals to Prayer. May you grow in faith and enjoy the lessons in Andersen's stories illuminated by *The Message*.

Mary K. Doyle
Geneva, Illinois

HANS CHRISTIAN ANDERSEN

SELECTIONS FROM

Thumbelina
The Snail and the Rosebush
The Steadfast Tin Soldier
The Wild Swans
The Ugly Duckling
A Real Princess
The Tinder Box
Shepherdess and Chimney Sweep
Little Ida's Flowers
The Emperor's New Clothes
The Snow Queen
The Flying Trunk
The Fellow Traveler
The Nightingale
The Beetle
Whatever the Old Man Does
The Darning Needle
Fortune's Overshoes
The Bronze Boar
The Bell

FIRST AID

As she did so she was frightened, for it seemed as if something was knocking inside there. It was the bird's heart. He was not dead; he was only numb with the cold. Now he had been warmed, and had come to life again.

In autumn all the swallows fly away to the warm countries; but if one happens to be belated, it gets so cold that it drops down as if dead, lies where it falls, and is covered by the cold snow.

Thumbelina trembled exceedingly, so startled was she; for the bird was large, very large compared with her, who was only an inch in height. But she took courage, laid the cotton closer round the poor Swallow, and brought a leaf that she had used as her own coverlet, and laid it over the bird's head.

The next night she crept out to him again, and now he was alive, but quite weak; he could only open his eyes for a moment and look at Thumbelina, as she stood before him with a bit of decayed wood in her hand, for she had no lantern.

"I thank you, pretty little child," said the sick Swallow; "I have been warmed. Soon my strength will return, and I shall be able to fly about again in the warm sunshine."

"Oh!" she said, "it is so cold outside. It is snowing and freezing. Stay in your warm bed, and I will nurse you."

THUMBELINA

Illuminated by The Message

FIRST AID

"A Samaritan traveling the road came on him. When he saw the man's condition, his heart went out to him. He gave him first aid, disinfecting and bandaging his wounds. Then he lifted him onto his donkey, led him to an inn, and made him comfortable. In the morning he took out two silver coins and gave them to the innkeeper, saying, 'Take good care of him. If it costs any more, put it on my bill—I'll pay you on my way back.'"

LUKE 10:33-35

GREATER GIFTS, GREATER RESPONSIBILITIES

"No!" said the Rosebush. "I bloomed in gladness, for I could not do otherwise, the sun was so warm and the air so refreshing. I drank of the clear dew, and of the heavy rain; I breathed, I lived! From the ground a strength rose up within me, from above a strength came down to me. I felt a happiness, always new, always great, and therefore I always had to put forth buds and flowers. That was my life. I could not do otherwise!"

"You have led a very easy life," said the Snail.

"Yes, you are right. Everything was given to me," said the Rosebush; "but still more was given to you! You are one of those deep, meditative natures, one of the highly gifted that will astonish the world."

"I have no such design at all," said the Snail. "The world is nothing to me! I have enough to do with myself, and I have enough in myself."

"But should not all of us here on earth give to others the best that is in us, bring what we can? Yes, it is true, I have given only roses! But you? You, who received so much, what have you given to the world? What will you give to it?"

THE SNAIL AND THE ROSEBUSH

Illuminated by The Message

GREATER GIFTS, GREATER RESPONSIBILITIES

The Master said, "Let me ask you: Who is the dependable manager, full of common sense, that the master puts in charge of his staff to feed them well and on time? He is a blessed man if when the master shows up he's doing his job. But if he says to himself, 'The master is certainly taking his time,' begins maltreating the servants and maids, throws parties for his friends, and gets drunk, the master will walk in when he least expects it, give him the thrashing of his life, and put him back in the kitchen peeling potatoes.

"The servant who knows what his master wants and ignores it, or insolently does whatever he pleases, will be thoroughly thrashed. But if he does a poor job through ignorance, he'll get off with a slap on the hand. Great gifts mean great responsibilities; greater gifts, greater responsibilities!"

LUKE 12:42-48

THE GIFT OF A HANDICAP

There were once five-and-twenty tin soldiers; they were brothers, for they had all been cast from an old tin spoon. They shouldered their muskets and looked straight before them; and their uniforms were splendid in red and blue. The first thing they heard in the world, when the lid was taken off the box in which they lay, were the words "Tin Soldiers!" shouted by a little boy, as he clapped his hands in glee. The soldiers had been given to him on his birthday, and now he joyfully set them out on the table. Each soldier was exactly like every other, except one, and he had but one leg. He had been cast last of all, and there had not been enough tin to finish him, but he stood as firm on his one leg as the others on their two; and he is the very one that became remarkable.

THE STEADFAST TIN SOLDIER

THE GIFT OF A HANDICAP

Because of the extravagance of those revelations, and so I wouldn't get a big head, I was given the gift of a handicap to keep me in constant touch with my limitations. Satan's angel did his best to get me down; what he in fact did was push me to my knees. No danger then of walking around high and mighty! At first I didn't think of it as a gift, and begged God to remove it. Three times I did that, and then he told me,

My grace is enough; it's all you need.
My strength comes into its own in your weakness.

Once I heard that, I was glad to let it happen. I quit focusing on the handicap and began appreciating the gift. It was a case of Christ's strength moving in on my weakness. Now I take limitations in stride, and with good cheer, these limitations that cut me down to size—abuse, accidents, opposition, bad breaks. I just let Christ take over! And so the weaker I get, the stronger I become.

2 CORINTHIANS 12:7-10

SALVATION BELONGS TO GOD

The Tin Soldier stood up to his neck in water, the boat sank deeper and deeper, the paper grew more and more limp. Then the water closed over the Soldier's head. He thought of the pretty little Dancer, and that he would never see her again; and in the Soldier's ears rang the song: "Farewell, farewell, thou warrior brave, For thou must die this day!"

Then the paper boat went to pieces, and the Tin Soldier fell through; but at that moment he was swallowed up by a great fish.

Oh, how dark it was! It was worse even than in the drain; and it was very narrow, too. But the Tin Soldier remained calm, and lay at full length, gripping his musket.

The fish rushed about, making the most fearful movements, and then became quite still. After a long time something suddenly flashed through it like a gleam of lightening. It was now quite light, and a voice exclaimed loudly, "The Tin Soldier!"

The fish had been caught, carried to market, and sold. It had been taken into the kitchen, where the cook had cut it open with a large knife. She seized the Soldier round the body with two fingers, and carried him into the living room. All were anxious to see the remarkable man that had traveled about inside of a fish; but the Tin Soldier was not at all proud.

THE STEADFAST TIN SOLDIER

Illuminated by The Message

SALVATION BELONGS TO GOD

"Ocean gripped me by the throat.
 The ancient Abyss grabbed me and held tight.
My head was all tangled in seaweed
 at the bottom of the sea where the mountains take root.
I was as far down as a body can go,
 and the gates were slamming shut behind me forever—
Yet you pulled me up from that grave alive,
 O GOD, my God!
When my life was slipping away,
 I remembered GOD,
And my prayer got through to you,
 made it all the way to your Holy Temple.
Those who worship hollow gods, god-frauds,
 walk away from their only true love.
But I'm worshiping you, GOD,
 calling out in thanksgiving!
And I'll do what I promised I'd do!
 Salvation belongs to GOD!"

Then GOD spoke to the fish, and it vomited up Jonah on the seashore.

JONAH 2:5-10

A PLAN TO CONTAIN THEM

Oh, these children were very, very happy! But thus it was not always to be.

Their father, who was king over all the land, married a wicked queen who was not at all kind to the poor children; they felt that on the very first day. There were great festivities at the castle, and the children played at visiting and having company. But instead of letting them have all the cakes and baked apples they could eat, as they were used to having, the queen gave them only some sand in a teacup, telling them they could make believe that it was something to eat.

The following week she sent little Elise into the country to live with some peasant people, and it did not take her long to make the king believe so many bad things of the boys that he cared no more about them.

"You shall fly out into the world and look after yourselves," said the wicked queen; "fly away as great voiceless birds!"

THE WILD SWANS

A PLAN TO CONTAIN THEM

A new king came to power in Egypt who didn't know Joseph. He spoke to his people in alarm, "There are way too many of these Israelites for us to handle. We've got to do something: Let's devise a plan to contain them, lest if there's a war they should join our enemies, or just walk off and leave us."

So they organized them into work-gangs and put them to hard labor under gang-foremen. They built the storage cities Pithom and Rameses for Pharaoh. But the harder the Egyptians worked them the more children the Israelites had—children everywhere! The Egyptians got so they couldn't stand the Israelites and treated them worse than ever, crushing them with slave labor. They made them miserable with hard labor—making bricks and mortar and back-breaking work in the fields. They piled on the work, crushing them under the cruel workload.

EXODUS 1:8-14

YOUR RIGHTEOUSNESS IS ON EVERYONE'S LIPS

The days went by, one just like the other. When the wind blew through the hedges outside the house, it whispered to the roses, "Who could be more beautiful than you?" The roses shook their heads and answered, "Elise!" And when the old woman sat in the doorway of a Sunday reading in her psalm-book, the wind turned the pages and said to the book, "Who could be more devout than you?" "Elise!" answered the book. And both the roses and the book of psalms spoke the exact truth.

THE WILD SWANS

Illuminated by The Message

YOUR RIGHTEOUSNESS IS ON EVERYONE'S LIPS

I lift you high in praise, my God, O my King!
  and I'll bless your name into eternity.

I'll bless you every day,
  and keep it up from now to eternity.

G<small>OD</small> is magnificent; he can never be praised enough.
  There are no boundaries to his greatness.

Generation after generation stands in awe of your work;
  each one tells stories of your mighty acts.

Your beauty and splendor have everyone talking;
  I compose songs on your wonders.

Your marvelous doings are headline news;
  I could write a book full of the details of your greatness.

The fame of your goodness spreads across the country;
  your righteousness is on everyone's lips.

PSALM 145:1-7

CONFIDENT IN YOUR VERDICT

The whole populace streamed out of the town gates to see the witch burned. A miserable horse drew the cart in which Elise was seated. They had put upon her a garment of course sackcloth, and all her wonderful long hair hung loose about her beautiful head. Her cheeks were deathly pale, and her lips moved softly, while her fingers unceasingly twisted the green flax. Even on the way to her death she did not abandon her unfinished work. The shirts lay completed at her feet and she was knitting the eleventh.

The populace scoffed at her. "See how the witch mutters. No psalm-book has she in her hands; no, there she sits with her loathsome sorcery. Tear it away from her, into a thousand pieces!"

The crowd pressed around her to destroy her work, but just then eleven white swans came flying and perched on the cart around her and flapped their great wings. The crowed gave way before them in terror.

"It is a sign from Heaven! She must be innocent!" they whispered but they dared not say it aloud.

THE WILD SWANS

Illuminated by The Message

CONFIDENT IN YOUR VERDICT

GOD! God! I am running to you for dear life;
   the chase is wild.
If they catch me, I'm finished:
   ripped to shreds by foes fierce as lions,
   dragged into the forest and left
   unlooked for, unremembered.

GOD, if I've done what they say—
   betrayed my friends,
   ripped off my enemies—
If my hands are really that dirty,
   let them get me, walk all over me,
   leave me flat on my face in the dirt.

Stand up, GOD; pit your holy fury
   against my furious enemies.
Wake up, God. My accusers have packed
   the courtroom; it's judgment time.
Take your place on the bench, reach for your gavel,
   throw out the false charges against me.
I'm ready, confident in your verdict:
   "Innocent."

PSALM 7:1-8

THEY ABUSE ME

And so they made themselves at home. But the poor Duckling that had been hatched out last and looked so ugly, was bitten and pushed and jeered at, and as much by the chickens as by the ducks.

"He is too big!" they all said.

The turkey cock, who had been born with spurs, and therefore thought himself an emperor, blew himself up like a ship in full sail, and bore straight down upon it; then he gobbled, and grew very red in the face. The poor Duckling did not know whether to stand or sit, and became very miserable, because it was so ugly and was scoffed at by the whole yard.

Thus the first day passed; and thereafter things became worse and worse. The poor Duckling was chased about by every one; even its brothers and sisters were quite unkind to it, and said, "If only the cat would catch you, you ugly creature!" And the mother said, "Would that you were far away!" and the ducks bit it, and the chickens pecked it, and the girl who had to feed the poultry kicked at it with her foot.

Then it ran away, flying over the hedge fence, and making the little birds in the bushes fly up in fear.

"That is because I am so ugly!" thought the Duckling. It shut its eyes, but kept running on.

THE UGLY DUCKLING

Illuminated by The Message

THEY ABUSE ME

"But now I'm the one they're after,
  mistreating me, taunting and mocking.
They abhor me, they abuse me.
  How dare those scoundrels—they spit in my face!
Now that God has undone me and left me in a heap,
  they hold nothing back. Anything goes.
They come at me from my blind side,
  trip me up, then jump on me while I'm down.
They throw every kind of obstacle in my path,
  determined to ruin me—
  and no one lifts a finger to help me!
They violate my broken body,
  trample through the rubble of my ruined life.
Terrors assault me—
  my dignity in shreds,
  salvation up in smoke.
"And now my life drains out,
  as suffering seizes and grips me hard.
Night gnaws at my bones;
  the pain never lets up.
I am tied hand and foot, my neck in a noose.
  I twist and turn.
Thrown facedown in the muck,
  I'm a muddy mess, inside and out."

JOB 30:9-19

BE A BLESSING AND GET A BLESSING

The Duckling felt quite glad because of all the misery and misfortune it had suffered, for now it could rightly value its happiness and all the splendor that surrounded it. And the great swans swam round it and stroked it with their bills.

Into the garden came little children, who threw bread and corn into the water. The youngest cried, "There is a new one!" and the other children shouted joyously, "Yes, a new one has arrived!" They clapped their hands and danced about, then ran to their father and mother. Bread and cake were thrown into the water, and all said, "The new one is the most beautiful of all! so young and handsome!" and the old swans bowed their heads before it.

Then it felt quite bashful, and hid its head under its wing, for it did not know what to think. It was very happy, and yet not at all proud, for a good heart is never proud or conceited. It thought how it had been persecuted and despised; and now it heard them saying that it was the most beautiful of all beautiful birds. Even the lilac bush bent its branches straight down into the water before it; and the sun shone warm and mild. Then it shook its feathers, lifted its slender neck, and cried joyously from the depths of its heart:

"I never dreamed of such happiness when I was still the Ugly Duckling!"

THE UGLY DUCKLING

BE A BLESSING AND GET A BLESSING

Summing up: Be agreeable, be sympathetic, be loving, be compassionate, be humble. That goes for all of you, no exceptions. No retaliation. No sharp-tongued sarcasm....bless—that's your job, to bless. You'll be a blessing and also get a blessing.

> *Whoever wants to embrace life*
> *and see the day fill up with good,*
> *Here's what you do:*
> *Say nothing evil or hurtful;*
> *Snub evil and cultivate good;*
> *run after peace for all you're worth.*
> *God looks on all this with approval,*
> *listening and responding well to what he's asked;*
> *But he turns his back*
> *on those who do evil things.*

If with heart and soul you're doing good, do you think you can be stopped? Even if you suffer for it, you're still better off. Don't give the opposition a second thought. Through thick and thin, keep your hearts at attention, in adoration before Christ, your Master. Be ready to speak up and tell anyone who asks why you're living the way you are, and always with the utmost courtesy. Keep a clear conscience before God so that when people throw mud at you, none of it will stick. They'll end up realizing that they're the ones who need a bath.

1 PETER 3:8-16

PURITY OF HEART

It was a princess who stood outside. But gracious, how she looked from the rain and the storm! The water streamed out of her hair and her clothes, it ran in at the toes of her shoes and out at the heels, and then she declared that she was a real princess.

"Well, we shall soon find out!" thought the old queen. Without saying a word, she went into the bedchamber, took all the bedclothes off the bed, and placed a single green pea on the bottom of the bed. Then she took twenty mattresses and piled them one on top of the other over the pea, and then piled twenty feather beds on top of the mattresses.

There the princess was to sleep that night.

In the morning they asked her how she had slept.

"Oh, wretchedly!" said the princess. "I have hardly closed my eyes all night long! Heaven knows what was in that bed! I have been lying on some hard thing, so that my whole body is black and blue with bruises! It is really terrible!"

When they saw at once that she was a real princess, for she had felt the pea through twenty mattresses and twenty feather beds. None but a real princess could have so tender a skin and be so easily bruised.

So the prince took her to be his wife, for now he knew he had found a real princess. The pea was placed in the museum of art, where it may still be seen if no one has carried it away.

A REAL PRINCESS

PURITY OF HEART

Distress that drives us to God does that. It turns us around. It gets us back in the way of salvation. We never regret that kind of pain. But those who let distress drive them away from God are full of regrets, end up on a deathbed of regrets.

And now, isn't it wonderful all the ways in which this distress has goaded you closer to God? You're more alive, more concerned, more sensitive, more reverent, more human, more passionate, more responsible. Looked at from any angle, you've come out of this with purity of heart. And that is what I was hoping for in the first place when I wrote the letter. My primary concern was not for the one who did the wrong or even the one wronged, but for you—that you would realize and act upon the deep, deep ties between us before God. That's what happened—and we felt just great.

2 CORINTHIANS 7:10-13

MONEY DECEIVES

What a quantity of money! The soldier threw away all the silver coins with which he had filled his pockets and his knapsack, and replaced them with gold; he filled even his boots and his cap, so that he could scarcely walk. Now, indeed, he had plenty of money. He put the dog back on the chest, slammed the door, and then called up through the tree, "Now pull me up, old witch."

"Are you bringing the tinder-box?" asked the witch.

"That's so!" exclaimed the soldier. "I forgot it completely." And back he went and found it.

The witch then drew him up, and there he stood on the highroad with pockets, boots, knapsack, and cap full of gold.

"What do you want with the tinder-box?" asked the soldier.

"That's nothing to you," replied the witch. "You have your money—now give me the tinder-box."

"Nonsense!" said the solder. "Tell me directly what you want with it, or I'll draw my sword and cut off your head."

"No!" cried the witch.

So the soldier struck off her head and there she lay. Then he tied up all his money in her apron, took it on his back like a sack, put the tinder-box in his pocket, and went straight off to the city.

THE TINDER BOX

Illuminated by The Message

MONEY DECEIVES

"Note well: Money deceives.
  The arrogant rich don't last.
They are more hungry for wealth
  than the grave is for cadavers.
Like death, they always want more,
  but the 'more' they get is dead bodies.
They are cemeteries filled with dead nations,
  graveyards filled with corpses.
Don't give people like this a second thought.
  Soon the whole world will be taunting them:

"'Who do you think you are—
  getting rich by stealing and extortion?
How long do you think
  you can get away with this?'
Indeed, how long before your victims wake up,
  stand up and make you the victim?
You've plundered nation after nation.
  Now you'll get a taste of your own medicine.
All the survivors are out to plunder you,
  a payback for all your murders and massacres."

HABAKKUK 2:5-8

LET'S RUN OFF TOGETHER

But the little Shepherdess wept and looked at her heart's best beloved, the porcelain Chimney Sweep.

"I think I will ask you," she said, "to take me with you out into the wide world, for here we cannot stay!"

"I want to do everything that you want to do!" said the little Chimney Sweep. "Let us go immediately. I know I can support you with my profession!"

"If we were only safely down off the table!" she said. "I shall not be happy until we are out in the wide world!"

He comforted her and showed her how she should put her little foot on the projecting points and the gilded foliage carved on the table leg. He also used his ladder to help her, and there they were, down on the floor. But when they looked over at the old cupboard there was such a commotion! All the carved stags stuck their heads farther out, raising their antlers and turning their necks. The Billy-Goat-Legs-Major-and Lieutenant-General-War-Commander-Sergeant jumped high in the air, and shouted to the old Chinaman, "They are running away! They are running away!"

SHEPHERDESS AND CHIMNEY SWEEP

Illuminated by The Message

LET'S RUN OFF TOGETHER

Kiss me—full on the mouth!
 Yes! For your love is better than wine,
 headier than your aromatic oils.
The syllables of your name murmur like a meadow brook.
 No wonder everyone loves to say your name!

Take me away with you! Let's run off together!
 An elopement with my King-Lover!
We'll celebrate, we'll sing,
 we'll make great music.
Yes! For your love is better than vintage wine.
 Everyone loves you—of course! And why not?

SONG OF SONGS 1:2-4

LEAVE YOUR COUNTRY

"Have you really the courage to go with me out into the wide world?" asked the Chimney Sweep. "Have you considered how great it is, and that we can never come back here again!"

"That I have!" she said.

The Chimney Sweep looked straight into her eyes, and then he said, "My way lies through the chimney! Have you really the courage to crawl with me through the stove, through the fire box, and through the stove pipe? Then we get out into the chimney and there I know how to get along. We climb so high that they cannot reach us, and farthest up is a hole that leads out to the wide world!"

Then he led her over to the door of the stove.

"It looks black!" she said, but still she went with him, through the fire box and through the stove pipe, where it was as dark as the blackest night.

SHEPHERDESS AND CHIMNEY SWEEP

LEAVE YOUR COUNTRY

God told Abram: "Leave your country, your family, and your father's home for a land that I will show you.

> I'll make you a great nation
> and bless you.
> I'll make you famous;
> you'll be a blessing.
> I'll bless those who bless you;
> those who curse you I'll curse.
> All the families of the Earth
> will be blessed through you."

So Abram left just as God said, and Lot left with him. Abram was seventy-five years old when he left Haran. Abram took his wife Sarai and his nephew Lot with him, along with all the possessions and people they had gotten in Haran, and set out for the land of Canaan and arrived safe and sound.

Abram passed through the country as far as Shechem and the Oak of Moreh. At that time the Canaanites occupied the land.

God appeared to Abram and said, "I will give this land to your children." Abram built an altar at the place God had appeared to him.

He moved on from there to the hill country east of Bethel and pitched his tent between Bethel to the west and Ai to the east. He built an altar there and prayed to God.

GENESIS 12:1-8

LOVE FOREVER

Then the Chimney Sweep and the little Shepherdess looked in such a distressed manner at the old Chinaman! They were afraid that he would nod, but that you know he could not do. And, besides, he found it unpleasant to tell a stranger that he had a rivet in the back of his neck. So the young porcelain people remained together and blessed grandfather's rivet and loved one another till they broke.

SHEPHERDESS AND CHIMNEY SWEEP

Illuminated by The Message

LOVE FOREVER

"I'm with him for good and I'll love him forever;
I've set him on high—he's riding high!
I've put Ocean in his one hand, River in the other;
he'll call out, 'Oh, my Father—my God,
my Rock of Salvation!'
Yes, I'm setting him apart
as the First of the royal line,
High King over all of earth's kings.
I'll preserve him eternally in my love,
I'll faithfully do all I so solemnly promised.
I'll guarantee his family tree
and underwrite his rule."

PSALM 89:25-29

STRIKE UP THE BAND

"I was out in that garden yesterday with my mother," said Ida. "But there were no leaves on the trees, and there was not a single flower left! Where are they? Last summer I saw so many!"

"They are inside the castle," said the Student. "You must know that as soon as the king and all the court ladies and gentlemen move to the city, the flowers immediately run up out of the garden and into the castle, and there they have such merry times! You just ought to see! The two most beautiful roses seat themselves on the throne. They are the king and queen. All the red cockscombs arrange themselves on each side, and bow. They are the chamberlains. Then all the most beautiful flowers come in, and the ball begins. The blue violets make believe they are naval cadets, and dance with the hyacinths and crocuses, which they call young ladies! The tulips and the large yellow lilies are elderly ladies, who watch over the younger set and take care that they conduct themselves properly!"

LITTLE IDA'S FLOWERS

STRIKE UP THE BAND

Hallelujah!
Sing to God a brand-new song,
*   praise him in the company of all who love him.*
Let all Israel celebrate their Sovereign Creator,
*   Zion's children exult in their King.*
Let them praise his name in dance;
*   strike up the band and make great music!*
And why? Because God delights in his people,
*   festoons plain folk with salvation garlands!*

Let true lovers break out in praise,
*   sing out from wherever they're sitting,*
Shout the high praises of God,
*   brandish their swords in the wild sword-dance—*
A portent of vengeance on the God-defying nations,
*   a signal that punishment's coming,*
Their kings chained and hauled off to jail,
*   their leaders behind bars for good,*
The judgment on them carried out to the letter
*   —and all who love God in the seat of honor!*
Hallelujah!

PSALM 149

DIVERSITY OF RESURRECTION GLORY

"Can the flowers in the botanical gardens also go out there? Are they able to travel that long distance?"

"Of course they can!" said the Student. "They can fly, if they want to! Have you not seen the beautiful butterflies, some red, some yellow, and some white, that look so much like flowers? That is what they once were; but they leaped from their stalks high in the air, and beat with their leaves as though they were little wings—and away they flew! And because they behaved themselves nicely, they were given permission to fly about in the daytime, too; they did not have to go home again and sit quiet on their stalks. And thus the leaves at last became real wings. That you have seen for yourself! It might be, however, that the flowers in the botanical gardens have never been out at the king's castle, or do not even know that there is such merriment there during the night. So now I am going to tell you something that will astonish the Professor of Botany next door very much. You know him, of course. When you go into his garden you must tell one of the flowers that a grand ball takes place at the castle. Then it will tell the news to all the others, and away they will fly. When the professor goes to walk in his garden, there will not be a single flower, and he will not be able to understand where they are.

LITTLE IDA'S FLOWERS

DIVERSITY OF RESURRECTION GLORY

Some skeptic is sure to ask, "Show me how resurrection works. Give me a diagram; draw me a picture. What does this 'resurrection body' look like?" If you look at this question closely, you realize how absurd it is. There are no diagrams for this kind of thing. We do have a parallel experience in gardening. You plant a "dead" seed; soon there is a flourishing plant. There is no visual likeness between seed and plant. You could never guess what a tomato would look like by looking at a tomato seed. What we plant in the soil and what grows out of it don't look anything alike. The dead body that we bury in the ground and the resurrection body that comes from it will be dramatically different.

You will notice that the variety of bodies is stunning. Just as there are different kinds of seeds, there are different kinds of bodies—humans, animals, birds, fish—each unprecedented in its form. You get a hint at the diversity of resurrection glory by looking at the diversity of bodies not only on earth but in the skies—sun, moon, stars—all these varieties of beauty and brightness. And we're only looking at pre-resurrection "seeds"—who can imagine what the resurrection "plants" will be like!

I CORINTHIANS 15:35-41

TALKING NONSENSE, NOISY NONSENSE

"Have you not seen how the flowers nod when the wind blows a little, and move all their green leaves? That is just as plain as if they talked!"

"Can the Professor understand the sign language?" asked Ida.

"Certainly he can! One morning he went down into his garden and saw a great stinging nettle make signs with its leaves to a pretty red carnation. 'You are so beautiful,' it said, 'and I love you very much!' But the Professor does not like such things, and struck the leaves off the nettle, for you see they are its fingers. But the thorny leaves stung him, and since that time he never dares touch a nettle."

"That is very amusing!" said little Ida, laughing.

"What nonsense to put in a child's head!" said the tiresome Councilor, who had come to pay a visit and was sitting on the sofa. He did not like the Student, and always grumbled when he saw him cutting out the queer, comical figures. Sometimes it was a man hanging on a gibbet and holding a heart in his hand, for he was a heart stealer; sometimes an old witch riding on a broomstick and carrying her husband on her nose. Such things the Councilor could not bear to see, and he would always say, as he did now, "What nonsense to put in a child's head! Nothing but stupid fancies!"

LITTLE IDA'S FLOWERS

TALKING NONSENSE, NOISY NONSENSE

Bildad from Shuhah was next to speak:

"How can you keep on talking like this?
  You're talking nonsense, and noisy nonsense at that.
Does God mess up?
  Does God Almighty ever get things backward?
It's plain that your children sinned against him—
  otherwise, why would God have punished them?
Here's what you must do—and don't put it off any longer:
  Get down on your knees before God Almighty.
If you're as innocent and upright as you say,
  it's not too late—he'll come running;
  he'll set everything right again, reestablish your fortunes.
Even though you're not much right now,
  you'll end up better than ever.

JOB 8:1-7

A RIGHT TIME FOR BIRTH AND ANOTHER FOR DEATH

When she got up next morning she hurried to the little table to see if the flowers were still there. She drew the curtains of the little bed aside and—yes, there lay all her flowers; but they were very withered, much more so than the day before. Sophy lay in the drawer, where she had put her; she looked very sleepy.

"Do you remember what you were to tell me?" said little Ida. But Sophy looked very stupid, and said not a single word.

"You are not good," said Ida; "and they all danced with you, too!" Then she took a little paper box on which beautiful birds were painted, opened it, and placed the dead flowers inside. "This shall be your pretty coffin," she said. "Later, when my cousins come over, they shall help bury you in the garden, so that you may grow up next summer and become more beautiful!"

LITTLE IDA'S FLOWERS

A RIGHT TIME FOR BIRTH AND ANOTHER FOR DEATH

There's an opportune time to do things, a right time for everything on the earth:

> *A right time for birth and another for death,*
> *A right time to plant and another to reap,*
> *A right time to kill and another to heal,*
> *A right time to destroy and another to construct,*
> *A right time to cry and another to laugh,*
> *A right time to lament and another to cheer,*
> *A right time to make love and another to abstain,*
> *A right time to embrace and another to part,*
> *A right time to search and another to count your losses,*
> *A right time to hold on and another to let go,*
> *A right time to rip out and another to mend,*
> *A right time to shut up and another to speak up,*
> *A right time to love and another to hate,*
> *A right time to wage war and another to make peace.*

ECCLESIASTES 3:1-8

PROUD AND ARROGANT

Many years ago there lived an Emperor who was so inordinately fond of fine new clothes that he paid out all his money for the sole purpose of being particularly well dressed. He cared nothing for his soldiers, he cared not a whit about the theater, or for driving in the park, except alone that he might show off his new clothes. He had a garment for every hour of the day, and just as they usually say of a king, "He is in the council chamber," they always said of this Emperor, "He is in his clothes cabinet."

The great city in which he lived was very gay, and every day visitors came in large numbers. One day two swindlers, who gave themselves out as weavers, arrived, saying that they knew how to weave the loveliest cloth that any one could imagine. Not only were the colors and the pattern something extraordinarily beautiful, but the clothes which were made of the cloth they wove had this wonderful property: they became invisible to every person who was unfit for his office or was too stupid for any use.

THE EMPEROR'S NEW CLOTHES

PROUD AND ARROGANT

This is what must be done: When he sits down on the throne of his kingdom, the first thing he must do is make himself a copy of this Revelation on a scroll, copied under the supervision of the Levitical priests. That scroll is to remain at his side at all times; he is to study it every day so that he may learn what it means to fear his GOD, living in reverent obedience before these rules and regulations by following them. He must not become proud and arrogant, changing the commands at whim to suit himself or making up his own versions. If he reads and learns, he will have a long reign as king in Israel, he and his sons.

DEUTERONOMY 17:18-20

A TRUE WITNESS NEVER LIES

"I should really like to know how they are getting on with the cloth!" thought the Emperor. But he had a slightly uneasy feeling in the region of his heart when he remembered that anyone who was stupid or was ill-suited to his office would not be able to see it. Of course he was sure that he needed to have no fears about himself, but still he wanted to send someone first, to see how matters stood.

Everybody in the whole city heard of the wonderful power that lay in the cloth, and everybody was eager to see how bad or how stupid his neighbor was.

"I will send my honest old minister to the weavers!" thought the emperor. "He can best see how the fabric looks for he has sense and intelligence, and no one fulfills his duties better than he!"

So the good old minister entered the room where the two rascals sat working at the empty looms.

"Mercy on us!" thought the old minister, opening his eyes wide, "I can't see a thing!"

But he didn't say it aloud.

Both the rascals begged him to come nearer and asked if he didn't think the pattern was beautiful and the colors lovely. Then they pointed to the empty frame and the poor old minister stared and stared and opened his eyes still wider. But he could see nothing, for there was nothing.

THE EMPEROR'S NEW CLOTHES

A TRUE WITNESS NEVER LIES

A true witness never lies;
    a false witness makes a business of it.

Cynics look high and low for wisdom—and never find it;
    the open-minded find it right on their doorstep!

Escape quickly from the company of fools;
    they're a waste of your time, a waste of your words.

The wisdom of the wise keeps life on track;
    the foolishness of fools lands them in the ditch.

The stupid ridicule right and wrong,
    but a moral life is a favored life.

The person who shuns the bitter moments of friends
    will be an outsider at their celebrations.

Lives of careless wrongdoing are tumbledown shacks;
    holy living builds soaring cathedrals.

There's a way of life that looks harmless enough;
    look again—it leads straight to hell.
Sure, those people appear to be having a good time,
    but all that laughter will end in heartbreak.

PROVERBS 14:5-13

YOU'LL ONLY LOOK FOOLISH YOURSELF

"Isn't it magnificent!" cried the two honest officials. "Just look, your majesty, what a splendid pattern! What wonderful colors!" and they pointed to the empty loom, for they thought the others surely would be able to see the cloth.

"What's this!" thought the emperor. "I don't see anything! This is dreadful! Am I stupid? Am I not fit to be Emperor? This is the most dreadful thing that could happen to me!"

"Oh, it is very beautiful indeed!" said the Emperor aloud. "It has my unqualified approval!"

He nodded his head in a satisfied manner and regarded the empty loom, for never would he say that he could not see anything. The whole retinue that had followed him stared and stared, but with no better results than the others had. Yet, although they saw nothing, they all exclaimed just as the Emperor had done, "Oh, it is very beautiful, indeed!" They advised him urgently to have clothes made of this splendid new cloth, and to wear them for the first time in the great procession which was soon to take place.

"That is magnificent, wonderful, superb!" was the cry that went from mouth to mouth. Everybody was perfectly pleased with the suggestion. Both the rascals were knighted by the Emperor, who gave each of them a cross to wear in his buttonhole and bestowed on them the title of Knight Weavers.

THE EMPEROR'S NEW CLOTHES

YOU'LL ONLY LOOK FOOLISH YOURSELF

We no more give honors to fools
  than pray for snow in summer or rain during harvest.

You have as little to fear from an undeserved curse
  as from the dart of a wren or the swoop of a swallow.

A whip for the racehorse, a tiller for the sailboat—
  and a stick for the back of fools!

Don't respond to the stupidity of a fool;
  you'll only look foolish yourself.

Answer a fool in simple terms
  so he doesn't get a swelled head.

You're only asking for trouble
  when you send a message by a fool.

A proverb quoted by fools
  is limp as a wet noodle.

Putting a fool in a place of honor
  is like setting a mud brick on a marble column.

To ask a moron to quote a proverb
  is like putting a scalpel in the hands of a drunk.

Hire a fool or a drunk
  and you shoot yourself in the foot.

PROVERBS 26:1-10

A GREAT PRETENSE OF SEEING

"My, how becoming they are! How well they fit!" said everybody. "What a pattern! What colors! What splendid garments they are!"

"They are waiting at the door with the canopy which is to be carried over your Majesty in the procession!" said the master-in-chief of ceremonies.

"Well, I am all ready, you see!" said the Emperor. "Don't they hang well?" And he turned around once more before the mirror! For he wanted it to appear as if he were looking closely at all his finery.

The chamberlains who were to carry the train fumbled on the floor with their hands as if they were picking it up. Then they walked along holding their hands high. They did not dare let it be known that they could see nothing.

And so the Emperor marched in the procession under the beautiful canopy and everybody on the street and in the windows cried out: "The Emperor's new clothes are peerless! What a beautiful train! How wonderfully they fit!"

No one would let it be known that he saw nothing, for that would have meant that he was unfit for his office, or else that he was very stupid. No clothes that the Emperor had ever worn had been such a success.

THE EMPEROR'S NEW CLOTHES

A GREAT PRETENSE OF SEEING

"It's well known that God isn't at the beck and call of sinners, but listens carefully to anyone who lives in reverence and does his will. That someone opened the eyes of a man born blind has never been heard of—ever. If this man didn't come from God, he wouldn't be able to do anything."

They said, "You're nothing but dirt! How dare you take that tone with us!" Then they threw him out in the street.

Jesus heard that they had thrown him out, and went and found him. He asked him, "Do you believe in the Son of Man?"

The man said, "Point him out to me, sir, so that I can believe in him."

Jesus said, "You're looking right at him. Don't you recognize my voice?"

"Master, I believe," the man said, and worshiped him.

Jesus then said, "I came into the world to bring everything into the clear light of day, making all the distinctions clear, so that those who have never seen will see, and those who have made a great pretense of seeing will be exposed as blind."

Some Pharisees overheard him and said, "Does that mean you're calling us blind?"

Jesus said, "If you were really blind, you would be blameless, but since you claim to see everything so well, you're accountable for every fault and failure."

JOHN 9:31-41

TWISTING THE TRUTH

"But he has nothing on!" said a little child.

"Just listen to the innocent!" said the child's father. But one person whispered to another what the child had said.

"He has nothing on; a little child says he has nothing on!"

"But he really hasn't anything on!" at last shouted all the people. The Emperor had a creepy feeling, for it seemed to him that they were right. But then he thought within himself, "I must carry the thing out and go through with the procession."

So he bore himself still more proudly, and the chamberlains walked along behind him carrying the train which was not there at all.

THE EMPEROR'S NEW CLOTHES

Illuminated by The Message

TWISTING THE TRUTH

Do you want to be counted wise, to build a reputation for wisdom? Here's what you do: Live well, live wisely, live humbly. It's the way you live, not the way you talk, that counts. Mean-spirited ambition isn't wisdom. Boasting that you are wise isn't wisdom. Twisting the truth to make yourselves sound wise isn't wisdom. It's the furthest thing from wisdom—it's animal cunning, devilish conniving. Whenever you're trying to look better than others or get the better of others, things fall apart and everyone ends up at the others' throats.

Real wisdom, God's wisdom, begins with a holy life and is characterized by getting along with others. It is gentle and reasonable, overflowing with mercy and blessings, not hot one day and cold the next, not two-faced. You can develop a healthy, robust community that lives right with God and enjoy its results only if you do the hard work of getting along with each other, treating each other with dignity and honor.

JAMES 3:13-18

BE WARY OF FALSE PREACHERS

He was an evil goblin. He was one of the very worst, for he was the demon himself.

One day he was in a very good humor, for he had made a mirror that had this peculiarity—everything good and beautiful that was reflected in it shrank to almost nothing, but whatever was worthless and ugly became prominent and looked worse than it really was. The loveliest landscapes, seen in this mirror, looked like boiled spinach, and the best people became hideous, or stood on their heads and had no bodies; their faces were so distorted as to be unrecognizable, and a single freckle appeared to spread out over nose and mouth. That was very amusing, the demon said. When a good, pious thought passed through any person's mind, it was shown in the mirror as a grin, so that the demon had to chuckle at his artful invention.

Those who visited the goblin school—for he kept a goblin school—declared everywhere that a wonder had been wrought. For now, they asserted, one could see, for the first time, how the world and the people in it really looked. They scurried about with the mirror, until there was not a country or a person in the whole world that had not appeared all twisted up in it.

THE SNOW QUEEN

BE WARY OF FALSE PREACHERS

"Be wary of false preachers who smile a lot, dripping with practiced sincerity. Chances are they are out to rip you off some way or other. Don't be impressed with charisma; look for character. Who preachers are is the main thing, not what they say. A genuine leader will never exploit your emotions or your pocketbook. These diseased trees with their bad apples are going to be chopped down and burned."

MATTHEW 7:15-20

A WILDLY WONDERFUL WORLD

How splendidly the roses bloomed that summer! The little girl had learned a psalm. In it something was said about roses, and in singing of roses, she thought of her own. She sang it to the little boy, and he sang with her: "Where roses blow in the flowery vale, There we the child Jesus shall hail."

And the little ones held each other by the hand, kissed the roses, looked into God's bright sunshine, and spoke to it as if the Christ-child were there. What splendid summer days those were! How beautiful it was out among the fresh rose-bushes, which seemed as if they would never stop blooming!

THE SNOW QUEEN

Illuminated by The Message

A WILDLY WONDERFUL WORLD

What a wildly wonderful world, GOD!
    You made it all, with Wisdom at your side,
    made earth overflow with your wonderful creations.
Oh, look—the deep, wide sea,
    brimming with fish past counting,
    sardines and sharks and salmon.
Ships plow those waters,
    and Leviathan, your pet dragon, romps in them.
All the creatures look expectantly to you
    to give them their meals on time.
You come, and they gather around;
    you open your hand and they eat from it.
If you turned your back,
    they'd die in a minute—
Take back your Spirit and they die,
    revert to original mud;
Send out your Spirit and they spring to life—
    the whole countryside in bloom and blossom.

The glory of GOD—let it last forever!
    Let GOD enjoy his creation!

PSALM 104:24-31

SOME UNSUSPECTING SOUL

Just then it was—the clock on the great church tower was striking five—that Kay said, "Ouch! I felt a sharp pain in my heart! And now something flew into my eye!"

The little girl put her arm about his neck; he blinked his eyes. No, there was nothing at all to be seen.

"I think it is gone!" said he; but it was not gone. It was just one of those glass fragments from that magic mirror—the wicked glass in which everything great and good which was mirrored in it seemed small and mean, and everything mean and wicked was reflected in such a way that every fault was noticeable at once. Poor little Kay had also received a splinter in his heart, and that would soon become like a lump of ice. It did not hurt him any longer now, but the splinter was still there.

"Why do you cry?" he asked. "You look ugly like that. There's nothing the matter with me! Oh, fie!" he suddenly exclaimed, "that rose is worm-eaten, and see, this one is quite crooked! After all, they're ugly roses. They're like the box in which they stand!"

And then he kicked the box hard and tore off the two roses.

"Kay, what are you doing!" cried the little girl.

When he saw how he frightened her, he tore off another rose, and then sprang in at his own window away from the amiable little Gerda.

THE SNOW QUEEN

Illuminated by The Message

SOME UNSUSPECTING SOUL

"When a defiling evil spirit is expelled from someone, it drifts along through the desert looking for an oasis, some unsuspecting soul it can bedevil. When it doesn't find anyone, it says, 'I'll go back to my old haunt.' On return it finds the person spotlessly clean, but vacant. It then runs out and rounds up seven other spirits more evil than itself and they all move in, whooping it up. That person ends up far worse off than if he'd never gotten cleaned up in the first place.

"That's what this generation is like: You may think you have cleaned out the junk from your lives and gotten ready for God, but you weren't hospitable to my kingdom message, and now all the devils are moving back in."

MATTHEW 12:43-45

ANGELS TO GUARD YOU WHEREVER YOU GO

It seemed to her that the waves nodded strangely. She took her red shoes, her dearest possession, and threw them both into the river; but they fell close to the shore, and the little wavelets brought them back to the land to her. It seemed as if the river would not take from her the things she treasured most, because it had not her little Kay; but she thought she had not thrown the shoes out far enough; so she crept into a boat that lay among the reeds, went to the farthest end, and threw the shoes out into the water. The boat was not tied, and the movement she made caused it to glide away from the shore. She noticed this, and hurried to get back; but before she reached the other end, the boat was a yard from the bank and was drifting fast.

Little Gerda was very much frightened and began to cry; but no one heard her except the sparrows, and they could not carry her to land; but they flew along by the shore, and sang, as if to console her, "Here we are! Here we are!" The boat drifted on with the stream and little Gerda, in her stocking feet, sat quite still. Her little red shoes floated along behind, but they could not come up with the boat, which made more headway.

It was very pretty along both shores. There were beautiful flowers, old trees, and slopes with sheep and cows; but not a human being was to be seen.

THE SNOW QUEEN

Illuminated by The Message

ANGELS TO GUARD YOU WHEREVER YOU GO

Say this: "God, you're my refuge.
I trust in you and I'm safe!"
That's right—he rescues you from hidden traps,
shields you from deadly hazards.
His huge outstretched arms protect you—
under them you're perfectly safe;
his arms fend off all harm.
Fear nothing—not wild wolves in the night,
not flying arrows in the day,
Not disease that prowls through the darkness,
not disaster that erupts at high noon.
Even though others succumb all around,
drop like flies right and left,
no harm will even graze you.
You'll stand untouched, watch it all from a distance,
watch the wicked turn into corpses.
Yes, because God's your refuge,
the High God your very own home,
Evil can't get close to you,
harm can't get through the door.
He ordered his angels
to guard you wherever you go.
If you stumble, they'll catch you;
their job is to keep you from falling.

PSALM 91:2-12

BABBLE

This Crow stopped a long time to look at her, nodding its head. Now it said, "Caw! Caw! Good-day! good-day!" It could not pronounce plainly, but it meant well toward the little girl, and asked where she was going all alone in the wide world. The word "alone" Gerda understood very well, and felt how much it expressed; she told the Crow the story of her whole life and fortune, and asked if it had not seen Kay.

And the Crow nodded very gravely, and said:

"That may be! That may be!"

"What? Do you think so?" cried the little girl; and she nearly squeezed the Crow to death and smothered it with kisses.

"Gently, gently!" said the Crow. "I think it may be the little Kay; but he must now certainly have forgotten you for the Princess."

"Does he live with a Princess?" asked Gerda.

"Yes; listen," said the Crow. "But it's so difficult for me to speak your language. If you know the crows' language, I can tell it much better."

"No, that I never learned," said Gerda; "but my grandmother understood it, and could speak it, too. I only wish I had learned it."

"No matter," said the Crow. "I will tell as well as I can, though that will be very badly."

THE SNOW QUEEN

BABBLE

At one time, the whole Earth spoke the same language. It so happened that as they moved out of the east, they came upon a plain in the land of Shinar and settled down.

They said to one another, "Come, let's make bricks and fire them well." They used brick for stone and tar for mortar.

Then they said, "Come, let's build ourselves a city and a tower that reaches Heaven. Let's make ourselves famous so we won't be scattered here and there across the Earth."

GOD came down to look over the city and the tower those people had built.

GOD took one look and said, "One people, one language; why, this is only a first step. No telling what they'll come up with next—they'll stop at nothing! Come, we'll go down and garble their speech so they won't understand each other." Then GOD scattered them from there all over the world. And they had to quit building the city. That's how it came to be called Babel, because there GOD turned their language into "babble." From there GOD scattered them all over the world.

GENESIS 11:1-9

LAVISH GIFTS ON THE POOR

And the Prince got out of his bed and let Gerda sleep in it. More than that he could not do. She folded her little hands, and thought, "How good men and animals are!" and then she closed her eyes and went quietly to sleep. All the dreams came flying in again, looking like angels, and they drew a little sled on which Kay sat nodding. But all this was only dreaming and therefore it ended as soon as she awoke.

The next day she was clothed from head to foot in velvet, and was asked to stay in the castle and have a good time. But all she asked for was a little carriage with a horse to draw it, and a pair of little boots; then she would ride away into the wide world and find Kay.

They dressed her beautifully and gave her not only boots but a muff; and when she was ready to depart, a coach made of pure gold stood before the door. Upon it shone like a star the coat-of-arms of the Prince and Princess. Coachmen, footmen, and outriders—for there were outriders, too—sat on horseback, with gold crowns on their heads. The Prince and Princess themselves helped her into the carriage and wished her all good fortune.

THE SNOW QUEEN

LAVISH GIFTS ON THE POOR

Hallelujah!
*Blessed man, blessed woman, who fear G*OD*,*
Who cherish and relish his commandments,
Their children robust on the earth,
And the homes of the upright—how blessed!
Their houses brim with wealth
And a generosity that never runs dry.
Sunrise breaks through the darkness for good people—
God's grace and mercy and justice!
The good person is generous and lends lavishly;
No shuffling or stumbling around for this one,
But a sterling and solid and lasting reputation.
Unfazed by rumor and gossip,
*Heart ready, trusting in G*OD*,*
Spirit firm, unperturbed,
Ever blessed, relaxed among enemies,
They lavish gifts on the poor—
A generosity that goes on, and on, and on.
An honored life! A beautiful life!
Someone wicked takes one look and rages,
Blusters away but ends up speechless.
There's nothing to the dreams of the wicked. Nothing.

PSALM 112

KEEP US SAFE

Then little Gerda said the Lord's Prayer. The cold was so severe that as she spoke the words of the prayer she could see her own breath, which came out of her mouth like smoke. Her breath became thicker and thicker, and the cloud formed itself into little bright angels, which grew and grew when they touched the earth. And all had helmets on their heads and shields and spears in their hands; their number increased, until when Gerda had finished her prayer a whole legion stood about her. They struck with their spears at the terrible snowflakes, shattering them in a thousand pieces; and little Gerda could then go ahead safely and happily. The angels patted her hands and feet, making her feel less cold, and she walked quickly forward toward the Snow Queen's palace.

THE SNOW QUEEN

Illuminated by The Message

KEEP US SAFE

So Jesus said, "When you pray, say,

Father,
Reveal who you are.
Set the world right.
Keep us alive with three square meals.
Keep us forgiven with you and forgiving others.
Keep us safe from ourselves and the Devil."

Then he said, "Imagine what would happen if you went to a friend in the middle of the night and said, 'Friend, lend me three loaves of bread. An old friend traveling through just showed up, and I don't have a thing on hand.'

"The friend answers from his bed, 'Don't bother me. The door's locked; my children are all down for the night; I can't get up to give you anything.'

"But let me tell you, even if he won't get up because he's a friend, if you stand your ground, knocking and waking all the neighbors, he'll finally get up and get you whatever you need.

"Here's what I'm saying:

Ask and you'll get;
Seek and you'll find;
Knock and the door will open."

LUKE 11:2-9

LIKE CHILDREN

But Gerda and Kay walked hand in hand, and wherever they went it was beautiful spring with foliage and flowers. The church bells rang, and they recognized the high steeples in the great city where they lived. They entered the city and went to the door of the grandmother's house, up the stairs, and into her room, where everything stood in its usual place. The big clock said "Tick! Tack!" and the hands were turning; but as Kay and Gerda entered the room they noticed that they had become grown-up people. The roses out on the roof-gutter were nodding in at the open window, and there stood the children's chairs. Kay and Gerda sat down on their little chairs, and held each other by the hand. The cold, empty splendor at the Snow Queen's had passed from their memory like a bad dream. Grandmother was sitting in God's bright sunshine, and reading aloud out of the Bible, "Except ye become as little children, ye shall not enter into the kingdom of heaven."

Kay and Gerda looked into each other's eyes, and all at once they understood the old song: "Where roses blow in the flowery vale, There we the child Jesus shall hail."

There they sat, both grown up and yet children—children in heart; and it was summer—warm, delightful summer.

THE SNOW QUEEN

LIKE CHILDREN

At about the same time, the disciples came to Jesus asking, "Who gets the highest rank in God's kingdom?"

For an answer Jesus called over a child, whom he stood in the middle of the room, and said, "I'm telling you, once and for all, that unless you return to square one and start over like children, you're not even going to get a look at the kingdom, let alone get in. Whoever becomes simple and elemental again, like this child, will rank high in God's kingdom. What's more, when you receive the childlike on my account, it's the same as receiving me."

MATTHEW 18:1-5

FANTASY STORIES AND FANCIFUL FAMILY TREES

"Thank you!" said the merchant's son. Then he went out into the woods, seated himself in his trunk, and flew up on the roof of the castle. Then he crept through the window into the room of the Princess.

She was lying asleep on the sofa and she was so beautiful that the merchant's son had to kiss her. She awoke at once and was very much frightened. But when the stranger told her that he was a Turkish deity who had come down to her through the air, she was very much pleased.

They sat down side by side, and he told her stories about her eyes. He told her they were beautiful, dusky lakes, and that her thoughts were swimming there like mermaids. And he talked to her about her forehead. It was a snowy mountain, he said, with the most splendid halls full of pictures. He told her about the stork that brings the dear little children.

Yes, those were fine stories! Then he asked the Princess if she would marry him, and she said "Yes" immediately.

THE FLYING TRUNK

FANTASY STORIES AND FANCIFUL FAMILY TREES

On my way to the province of Macedonia, I advised you to stay in Ephesus. Well, I haven't changed my mind. Stay right there on top of things so that the teaching stays on track. Apparently some people have been introducing fantasy stories and fanciful family trees that digress into silliness instead of pulling the people back into the center, deepening faith and obedience.

The whole point of what we're urging is simply love—love uncontaminated by self-interest and counterfeit faith, a life open to God. Those who fail to keep to this point soon wander off into cul-de-sacs of gossip. They set themselves up as experts on religious issues, but haven't the remotest idea of what they're holding forth with such imposing eloquence.

It's true that moral guidance and counsel need to be given, but the way you say it and to whom you say it are as important as what you say. It's obvious, isn't it, that the law code isn't primarily for people who live responsibly, but for the irresponsible, who defy all authority, riding roughshod over God, life, sex, truth, whatever! They are contemptuous of this great Message I've been put in charge of by this great God.

I TIMOTHY 1:3-11

PRETENTIOUS EGOS BROUGHT DOWN TO EARTH

So he bought rockets and fire-crackers and every kind of fireworks you could imagine, put them all into his trunk, and flew up into the air.

Whizz! How they sputtered and flared, and how they popped! All the Turks hopped in the air and their slippers flew about their ears; such a sight they had never witnessed before. Now they could see for themselves that it was a real Turkish deity who was to marry the Princess.

As soon as the merchant's son landed in the woods again with his trunk he decided to go into the city to hear what an impression he had made. It was quite natural that he should want to do this.

But what stories people do tell! Everyone whom he asked about it had seen it in a different way; but one and all thought it fine....

On the following day he was to be married.

He went back to the forest to seat himself in his trunk. But what had become of it? A spark from the fireworks had set fire to it, and the trunk had burned to ashes. He could not fly any more, and could not go to his bride.

THE FLYING TRUNK

PRETENTIOUS EGOS BROUGHT DOWN TO EARTH

People with a big head are headed for a fall,
 pretentious egos brought down a peg.
It's GOD alone at front-and-center
 on the Day we're talking about,
The Day that GOD-of-the-Angel-Armies
 is matched against all big-talking rivals,
 against all swaggering big names;
Against all giant sequoias
 hugely towering,
 and against the expansive chestnut;
Against Kilimanjaro and Annapurna,
 against the ranges of Alps and Andes;
Against every soaring skyscraper,
 against all proud obelisks and statues;
Against ocean-going luxury liners,
 against elegant three-masted schooners.
The swelled big heads will be punctured bladders,
 the pretentious egos brought down to earth,
Leaving GOD alone at front-and-center
 on the Day we're talking about.

And all those sticks and stones
 dressed up to look like gods
 will be gone for good.

ISAIAH 2:11-18

YOUR FUTURE IN HEAVEN

The following week the dead man was buried. John walked close behind the coffin. No more was he to see his good, kind father, who had loved him so much. He heard the earth fall on the coffin. Now he could see only a small corner of it, and with the next shovelful of earth that too was covered. Then it seemed to John as if his heart would burst with sorrow. Those standing around the grave sang a psalm, and it sounded so beautiful that tears filled John's eyes. He wept, and his tears eased his sorrow. The sun shone brightly on the green trees as if to say: "Do not be so sad, John! Can you not see how beautifully blue the sky is? Your father is up yonder, praying to God that you may always prosper!"

"I will always be good," said John; "for then I shall go to heaven to my father. What happiness it will be to see one another again! How much there will be to tell him! And he will show me so many things, and teach me so much of the joy and beauty of heaven, just as he used to teach me here on earth. Oh, What happiness it will be!"

THE FELLOW TRAVELER

YOUR FUTURE IN HEAVEN

Our prayers for you are always spilling over into thanksgivings. We can't quit thanking God our Father and Jesus our Messiah for you! We keep getting reports on your steady faith in Christ, our Jesus, and the love you continuously extend to all Christians. The lines of purpose in your lives never grow slack, tightly tied as they are to your future in heaven, kept taut by hope.

The Message is as true among you today as when you first heard it. It doesn't diminish or weaken over time. It's the same all over the world. The Message bears fruit and gets larger and stronger, just as it has in you. From the very first day you heard and recognized the truth of what God is doing, you've been hungry for more. It's as vigorous in you now as when you learned it from our friend and close associate Epaphras. He is one reliable worker for Christ! I could always depend on him. He's the one who told us how thoroughly love had been worked into your lives by the Spirit.

COLOSSIANS 1:3-8

HE JUMPED TO HIS FEET AND WALKED

The sun was already high when they sat down together under a large tree to eat their breakfast. Just then an old woman came up, leaning on a crutch. On her back she carried a bundle of sticks that she had gathered in the forest. Her apron was fastened up, and John could see the ends of three large bundles of fern and willow switches that she carried in it. When she was close to John and his companion her foot slipped and she fell with a loud shriek; for the poor old woman had broken her leg.

John would have carried her to her home at once, but the stranger opened his knapsack and took out a jar, saying that it contained an ointment which would make her leg well and strong immediately, so that she would be able to walk home by herself and as firmly and well as if she had never broken her leg. But in return he wanted her to give him the three bundles of switches she had in her apron.

"That would be paying well!" said the old woman, nodding her head strangely. She did not like to part with her switches, but neither was it pleasant to lie there with a broken leg. So she gave him the switches, and as soon as he had rubbed on the ointment the old woman got up and walked much better than she had been able to walk before. And it was all the work of that ointment. Such ointment was not to be had at any druggist's!

THE FELLOW TRAVELER

HE JUMPED TO HIS FEET AND WALKED

One day at three o'clock in the afternoon, Peter and John were on their way into the Temple for prayer meeting. At the same time there was a man crippled from birth being carried up. Every day he was set down at the Temple gate, the one named Beautiful, to beg from those going into the Temple. When he saw Peter and John about to enter the Temple, he asked for a handout. Peter, with John at his side, looked him straight in the eye and said, "Look here." He looked up, expecting to get something from them.

Peter said, "I don't have a nickel to my name, but what I do have, I give you: In the name of Jesus Christ of Nazareth, walk!" He grabbed him by the right hand and pulled him up. In an instant his feet and ankles became firm. He jumped to his feet and walked.

The man went into the Temple with them, walking back and forth, dancing and praising God. Everybody there saw him walking around and praising God. They recognized him as the one who sat begging at the Temple's Gate Beautiful and rubbed their eyes, astonished, scarcely believing what they were seeing.

The man threw his arms around Peter and John, ecstatic. All the people ran up to where they were at Solomon's Porch to see it for themselves.

ACTS 3:1-11

DRY BONES

"Come in," said the old king when John knocked at the door. John opened it, and the old king, in his dressing gown and embroidered slippers, came to meet him. His golden crown was on his head, his scepter in one hand and his golden ball in the other.

"Wait a moment!" he said, tucking the golden ball under his arm so as to be able to shake hands with John. But when he heard that John was a suitor he began to cry so bitterly that both the ball and the scepter fell to the floor, and he had to dry his eyes with the sleeve of his dressing gown. Poor old king!

"Don't do it!" he said. "You will fail, like all the others. Just look at this!" He took John out into the princess' garden. It was a terrible sight, indeed! In every tree hung three or four princes, who had courted the princess but had not been able to guess the things she asked them. At every breeze the bones rattled so that the little birds had been frightened away and never dared come into the garden. All the flowers were staked up with human bones, and in the flower pots were grinning skulls. That was indeed a nice garden for a princess to have!

"Here you see!" said the old king. "Your fate will be just like that of all the others you see here. So please give up your intention! You will make me very unhappy if you do not, for I take it so much to heart!"

THE FELLOW TRAVELER

DRY BONES

There were bones all over the plain—dry bones, bleached by the sun.

GOD said to me, "Son of man, can these bones live?"

I said, "Master GOD, only you know that."

He said to me, "Prophesy over these bones: 'Dry bones, listen to the Message of GOD!'"

GOD, the Master, told the dry bones, "Watch this: I'm bringing the breath of life to you and you'll come to life. I'll attach sinews to you, put meat on your bones, cover you with skin, and breathe life into you. You'll come alive and you'll realize that I am GOD!"

I prophesied just as I'd been commanded. As I prophesied, there was a sound and, oh, rustling! The bones moved and came together, bone to bone. I kept watching. Sinews formed, then muscles on the bones, then skin stretched over them. But they had no breath in them.

He said to me, "Prophesy to the breath. Prophesy, son of man. Tell the breath, 'GOD, the Master, says, Come from the four winds. Come, breath. Breathe on these slain bodies. Breathe life!'"

So I prophesied, just as he commanded me. The breath entered them and they came alive! They stood up on their feet, a huge army.

EZEKIEL 37:2-10

SING FOR JOY

Then the Nightingale sang, and so enchantingly that the tears came into the Emperors' eyes and ran down over his cheeks. The Nightingale sang a second time, and still more sweetly, and the song went straight to the heart. The Emperor was so well pleased that he said the Nightingale should have his golden slipper to wear around its neck. But the Nightingale thanked him and said that it had already received sufficient reward.

"I have seen tears in the Emperor's eyes—that is rich compensation. An Emperor's tears have a peculiar power. I am rewarded enough!" And again its throat trembled and there was a glorious burst of song.

"That is the sweetest coquetry I ever saw!" said the ladies who stood round, and then they held water in their mouths so as to gurgle when anyone spoke to them, thinking that by these means they could equal the Nightingale. The lackeys and ladies-in-waiting expressed themselves as perfectly satisfied; and that meant a great deal, for they of all people are the most difficult to please.

THE NIGHTINGALE

SING FOR JOY

What a beautiful home, GOD-of-the-Angel-Armies!
I've always longed to live in a place like this,
Always dreamed of a room in your house,
where I could sing for joy to God-alive!

Birds find nooks and crannies in your house,
sparrows and swallows make nests there.
They lay their eggs and raise their young,
singing their songs in the place where we worship.
GOD-of-the-Angel-Armies! King! God!
How blessed they are to live and sing there!

PSALM 84:1-4

DON'T FALL FOR IT

And so the artificial bird had to sing again. This was the thirty-fourth time that they had listened to the same piece. They did not yet quite know it by heart, for it was so very difficult. The concert master praised the bird extravagantly. He declared that it was better than the real Nightingale, not only in the matter of its plumage and the many beautiful diamonds, but of the works as well.

"For you see, ladies and gentlemen, and above all, your Imperial Majesty, with a real Nightingale one can never calculate what is coming, but in this artificial bird everything is certain. One can explain it; one can open it and make people understand where the waltzes come from, how they go, and how one note follows another."

"Those are my own ideas, exactly," everyone said.

THE NIGHTINGALE

DON'T FALL FOR IT

"If anyone tries to flag you down, calling out, 'Here's the Messiah!' or points, 'There he is!' don't fall for it. Fake Messiahs and lying preachers are going to pop up everywhere. Their impressive credentials and dazzling performances will pull the wool over the eyes of even those who ought to know better. But I've given you fair warning.

"So if they say, 'Run to the country and see him arrive!' or, 'Quick, get downtown, see him come!' don't give them the time of day. The Arrival of the Son of Man isn't something you go to see. He comes like swift lightning to you! Whenever you see crowds gathering, think of carrion vultures circling, moving in, hovering over a rotting carcass. You can be quite sure that it's not the living Son of Man pulling in those crowds."

MATTHEW 24:23-28

A TIME OF RECKONING

The poor Emperor could scarcely breathe; it was just as if something weighted heavily upon his chest. He opened his eyes, and then he saw that it was Death that sat on his breast. He had put on the Emperor's golden crown, and in one hand he held the Emperor's sword, and in the other, his beautiful banner. All around, from among the folds of the splendid velvet curtains, strange heads peered, some evil and repulsive, others beautiful and kindly. These were all the Emperor's bad and good deeds, that stood before him now when Death sat upon his breast.

"Do you remember this?" whispered one. "Do you remember that?" said another, and they told him of so many things that the perspiration stood out on his forehead.

"I never knew that!" said the Emperor. "Give me music! music! Sound the great Chinese drums," he cried, "so that I may not hear all that they are saying!"

But they continued speaking, and Death nodded like a Chinaman to all that was said.

THE NIGHTINGALE

Illuminated by The Message

A TIME OF RECKONING

"There's nothing done or said that can't be forgiven. But if you deliberately persist in your slanders against God's Spirit, you are repudiating the very One who forgives. If you reject the Son of Man out of some misunderstanding, the Holy Spirit can forgive you, but when you reject the Holy Spirit, you're sawing off the branch on which you're sitting, severing by your own perversity all connection with the One who forgives.

"If you grow a healthy tree, you'll pick healthy fruit. If you grow a diseased tree, you'll pick worm-eaten fruit. The fruit tells you about the tree.

"You have minds like a snake pit! How do you suppose what you say is worth anything when you are so foul-minded? It's your heart, not the dictionary, that gives meaning to your words. A good person produces good deeds and words season after season. An evil person is a blight on the orchard. Let me tell you something: Every one of these careless words is going to come back to haunt you. There will be a time of Reckoning. Words are powerful; take them seriously. Words can be your salvation. Words can also be your damnation."

MATTHEW 12:31-37

AN ARROGANT CYNIC

"Ruffian!" said the Beetle. Then he went outside a little way and thus came into a beautiful little flower garden, fragrant with roses and lavender.

"How lovely it is here!" said one of the little lady-birds which flew about with black dots on their strong red shields. "How sweet it smells and how pretty it is here!"

"I am used to better things," said the Beetle. "Do you call this place pretty? Why, there is not even a dung heap."

And then he continued on his way, into the shade of a large gillyflower on the stalk of which crawled a caterpillar.

"Oh, how lovely the world is!" said the caterpillar. "The sun is so nice and warm! Everything is so enjoyable! And finally I shall fall asleep and die, as they call it; then I shall wake up as a butterfly!"

"What notions you have!" said the Beetle. "Flutter about like a butterfly, indeed! I come from the emperor's stable, but no one there, not even the emperor's favorite horse who wears my cast-off gold shoes, has such crazy notions. Get wings! Fly! Indeed! Yes, now let us fly!"

And then away flew the Beetle. "I do not want to feel vexed, but still, I am vexed."

THE BEETLE

Illuminated by The Message

AN ARROGANT CYNIC

If you reason with an arrogant cynic,
  you'll get slapped in the face;
    confront bad behavior and get a kick in the shins.
So don't waste your time on a scoffer;
    all you'll get for your pains is abuse.
But if you correct those who care about life,
    that's different—they'll love you for it!
Save your breath for the wise—they'll be wiser for it;
    tell good people what you know—they'll profit from it.
Skilled living gets its start in the Fear-of-God,
    insight into life from knowing a Holy God.
It's through me, Lady Wisdom, that your life deepens,
    and the years of your life ripen.
Live wisely and wisdom will permeate your life;
    mock life and life will mock you.

PROVERBS 9:7-12

BE COURTEOUSLY REVERENT TO ONE ANOTHER

"Yes, but I traded the hen for a sack of rotten apples!"

"Now I positively must kiss you!" said the woman. "Thank you, my own dear husband! Now I will tell you something. When you were gone I thought of making a real good meal for you; egg pancake with onions. I had the eggs. But I had no onions Then I went over to the schoolmaster's. There they have leek in their garden, I know. But the wife is so stingy! I asked if I could borrow an onion. 'Borrow?' she said. 'Nothing grows in our garden, not even a rotten apple, and you cannot lend to me even that!' Now I can lend her ten, yes, even a whole sackful! That's a fine joke, old man!" and she kissed him right on the mouth.

"I like that!" said the Englishman. "Always downhill and yet always contented! It's worth the money!" And they paid a bushel of gold coins to the peasant who had not been scolded, but kissed.

It certainly always pays when the wife sees and declares that her old man is wise and always does the right thing.

WHATEVER THE OLD MAN DOES

Illuminated by The Message

BE COURTEOUSLY REVERENT TO ONE ANOTHER

Out of respect for Christ, be courteously reverent to one another.

Wives, understand and support your husbands in ways that show your support for Christ. The husband provides leadership to his wife the way Christ does to his church, not by domineering but by cherishing. So just as the church submits to Christ as he exercises such leadership, wives should likewise submit to their husbands.

Husbands, go all out in your love for your wives, exactly as Christ did for the church—a love marked by giving, not getting. Christ's love makes the church whole. His words evoke her beauty. Everything he does and says is designed to bring the best out of her, dressing her in dazzling white silk, radiant with holiness. And that is how husbands ought to love their wives. They're really doing themselves a favor—since they're already "one" in marriage.

No one abuses his own body, does he? No, he feeds and pampers it. That's how Christ treats us, the church, since we are part of his body. And this is why a man leaves father and mother and cherishes his wife. No longer two, they become "one flesh."

EPHESIANS 5:21-31

NOT A WORD OF BOASTING

"Yes, I used to live in a box in a young lady's room," said the Darning Needle, "and the young lady was a cook. She had five fingers on each hand, and anything so conceited as those five fingers I have never known. And yet the only reason for their existence was to hold me, to take me out of my box, and to lay me back in my box!"

"Did they shine in any way?" asked the bit of Broken Bottle.

"Shine!" said the Darning Needle. "No, they were very dull, and so conceited! They were five brothers, all born 'Fingers.' They held themselves upright, one against the other, though they were of different lengths. The outside one, Thumbkin, was short and fat. He marched out of line, and besides, he had but one joint in his back. He could bow only once, but he said that, if he were chopped off a person, the entire man would be ruined for military service. Pointer, the second finger, also known as 'Lick Dish,' got into the sweet and the sour, pointed at the sun and the moon, and was the one that pressed down on the pen when the Fingers wrote. Longman looked over the heads of all the others. Ringman went about with a gold ring about his stomach, and Little Man did nothing at all, and that was what he was proud of. Bragging and boasting it was, and nothing but bragging and boasting; and then I went into the wash!"

THE DARNING NEEDLE

Illuminated by The Message

NOT A WORD OF BOASTING

Nothing and no one is holy like GOD,
  no rock mountain like our God.
Don't dare talk pretentiously—
  not a word of boasting, ever!
For GOD knows what's going on.
  He takes the measure of everything that happens.
The weapons of the strong are smashed to pieces,
  while the weak are infused with fresh strength.
The well-fed are out begging in the streets for crusts,
  while the hungry are getting second helpings.
The barren woman has a houseful of children,
  while the mother of many is bereft.

1 SAMUEL 2:2-5

DON'T LET ME FALL INTO BAD COMPANY

"Where am I?" he asked, and his head felt dizzy when he thought of it.

"We'll drink calaret! Mead and Bremen beer!" cried one of the guests, "and you shall drink with us!"

Two girls then came in. One of them wore a cap of two colors. They filled the glasses and curtsied to the guests. An icy shiver ran down the Councilor's back.

"What in the world is this! What is this!" he cried. But he had to drink with them. They took entire possession of the good man. He was in complete despair, and when one of them said he was drunk, he had not the least doubt that the fellow was right. All he asked was that they would get him a droshky (the Russian word used in Denmark for cab or carriage); and then they thought he was talking Russian.

Never had he been in such rough and vulgar company. One would think the country had returned to heathendom, was his silent comment. Just then the idea came to him to get under the table, crawl to the door, and then wait for a chance to slip out. But when he reached the exit, the others discovered his intention, seized him by the legs, and then, to his great good fortune, the Overshoes came off—and with them, the whole enchantment.

FORTUNE'S OVERSHOES

Illuminated by The Message

DON'T LET ME FALL INTO BAD COMPANY

God, come close. Come quickly!
  Open your ears—it's my voice you're hearing!
Treat my prayer as sweet incense rising;
  my raised hands are my evening prayers.

Post a guard at my mouth, God,
  set a watch at the door of my lips.
Don't let me so much as dream of evil
  or thoughtlessly fall into bad company.
And these people who only do wrong—
  don't let them lure me with their sweet talk!
May the Just One set me straight,
  may the Kind One correct me,
Don't let sin anoint my head.
  I'm praying hard against their evil ways!
Oh, let their leaders be pushed off a high rock cliff;
  make them face the music.
Like a rock pulverized by a maul,
  let their bones be scattered at the gates of hell.

But God, dear Lord,
  I only have eyes for you.
Since I've run for dear life to you,
  take good care of me.
Protect me from their evil scheming,
  from all their demonic subterfuge.

PSALM 141:1-9

ENJOY THE WIFE YOU MARRIED

There he stood upstairs in the Lieutenant's room, his fingers holding a little pink sheet of paper, upon which was a poem—a poem by Mr. Lieutenant himself. For what man has not once in his life had a poetic moment, when just to write down one's thoughts brings the verses!

People write such verses when they are in love, but a prudent man does not have them printed. Lieutenant, love, and necessity, that is a triangle, or, as good—the half of Fortune's broken die. The Lieutenant felt this way about it, too, and he laid his head on the window sill and sighed very deeply.

"The poor Watchman out on the street is far happier than I! He does not know what I call longing! He has a home, a wife and children, who weep when he grieves, and rejoice when he rejoices! Oh, I should be happier than I am, could I change into him completely, for he is happier than I!"

At that moment the Watchman was again the Watchman, for it was because of the Overshoes that he had become Lieutenant. But, as we have seen, he then felt still less satisfied and would, nevertheless rather be what he really was.

So the Watchman was again watchman.

"That was an ugly dream!" he said, "but rather funny, anyhow. I thought I was the Lieutenant up yonder and that it wasn't anything pleasant by any means. I missed mother and the little ones, who are ready to stifle me with kisses.

FORTUNE'S OVERSHOES

Illuminated by The Message

ENJOY THE WIFE YOU MARRIED

Do you know the saying, "Drink from your own rain barrel,
*   draw water from your own spring-fed well"?*
It's true. Otherwise, you may one day come home
*   and find your barrel empty and your well polluted.*

Your spring water is for you and you only,
*   not to be passed around among strangers.*
Bless your fresh-flowing fountain!
*   Enjoy the wife you married as a young man!*
Lovely as an angel, beautiful as a rose—
*   don't ever quit taking delight in her body.*
*   Never take her love for granted!*

PROVERBS 5:15-19

TRUSTING IN OUR OWN STRENGTH

One of the young volunteer assistants, of whom it could be said only in a physical sense that his head was thick, had the watch that evening. The rain was pouring down. But in spite of such hindrances, the young man was determined to get out. He would be gone only a quarter of an hour; and that was not worth mentioning to the gatekeeper, he thought, when a man could so easily slip out between the iron bars. Near by lay the overshoes that the Watchman had forgotten to take with him. The thought did not for an instant occur to the Assistant that they were the Fortune's Overshoes. However, they would be very nice to wear in rainy weather; so he put them on.

Now the question was, whether he could squeeze through the bars of the gate. He had never tried it before. He reached the fence and stood there.

"How I wish I had my head outside!" he said to himself; and immediately, although his head was very large and thick, it slipped through easily and without mishap. Just depend upon the Overshoes! But now he had to get the rest of his body out and there he stood.

"I'm too fat!" he said. "I thought the head would have been the hardest to get through! I see I am not going to get out."

Then he wanted to pull his head back quickly, but he could not. He could move his neck without discomfort, but that was all. At first he felt angry; then his spirits sank into his boots.

FORTUNE'S OVERSHOES

TRUSTING IN OUR OWN STRENGTH

We don't want you in the dark, friends, about how hard it was when all this came down on us in Asia province. It was so bad we didn't think we were going to make it. We felt like we'd been sent to death row, that it was all over for us. As it turned out, it was the best thing that could have happened. Instead of trusting in our own strength or wits to get out of it, we were forced to trust God totally—not a bad idea since he's the God who raises the dead! And he did it, rescued us from certain doom. And he'll do it again, rescuing us as many times as we need rescuing. You and your prayers are part of the rescue operation—I don't want you in the dark about that either. I can see your faces even now, lifted in praise for God's deliverance of us, a rescue in which your prayers played such a crucial part.

2 CORINTHIANS 1:8-11

A NEW HEART

That was enough for the Overshoes! The hospital Assistant became a thought; and then began a very unusual journey right through the hearts of the first row of spectators. The first heart he passed through was a lady's. But he immediately thought he was in the Orthopaedic Institute, where the doctors straighten out deformities. He was in the room where plaster casts of the deformed limbs hang on the walls. The difference was that at the Institute the casts are made when the patient comes in, but here in this lady's heart they were taken and preserved when the good persons were away. They were casts of the faults and defects of lady friends that were here preserved.

Quickly he passed into another lady's heart, but this appeared to him like a great holy church. The white dove of innocence fluttered over the altar. How gladly he would have knelt there, but away he had to go, into the next heart. He could still hear the tone of the organ, however, and he felt that he had become a new and better man, and not unworthy to enter the next sanctuary. This was a poor attic room in which lay a sick mother. Through the open window came God's warm sunshine; lovely roses nodded from the little wooden box on the roof, and two sky-blue birds sang joyously, while the sick mother prayed for blessings on her daughter.

FORTUNE'S OVERSHOES

A NEW HEART

"For here's what I'm going to do: I'm going to take you out of these countries, gather you from all over, and bring you back to your own land. I'll pour pure water over you and scrub you clean. I'll give you a new heart, put a new spirit in you. I'll remove the stone heart from your body and replace it with a heart that's God-willed, not self-willed. I'll put my Spirit in you and make it possible for you to do what I tell you and live by my commands. You'll once again live in the land I gave your ancestors. You'll be my people! I'll be your God!"

EZEKIEL 36:24-28

SEIZE LIFE!

In the avenue he met an acquaintance, a young poet, who told him that he was going to start next day on his summer outing.

"What! Are you off again!" said the Copying Clerk. "You certainly are a free and happy man. You can fly wherever you please, while the rest of us are chained by the leg!"

"But the chain is fastened to the bread tree!" laughed the Poet. "You do not need to think of tomorrow; and when you get old you get a pension!"

"But you are better off, anyway!" said the Copying Clerk; "It must be a pleasure to sit and write poetry! All the world tells you nice agreeable things, and, moreover, you are your own master! You ought to try sitting in the courtroom and working with the trivial matters that come up there!"

FORTUNE'S OVERSHOES

SEIZE LIFE!

Seize life! Eat bread with gusto,
Drink wine with a robust heart.
Oh yes—God takes pleasure in your pleasure!
Dress festively every morning.
Don't skimp on colors and scarves.
Relish life with the spouse you love
Each and every day of your precarious life.
Each day is God's gift. It's all you get in exchange
For the hard work of staying alive.
Make the most of each one!
Whatever turns up, grab it and do it. And heartily!
This is your last and only chance at it,
For there's neither work to do nor thoughts to think
In the company of the dead,
   where you're most certainly headed.

ECCLESIASTES 9:7-10

BELIEVE IN THE LIGHT

"Hm! Hm!" said the Copying Clerk, seating himself on a bench. His thoughts were vivid, his heart so impressionable. Without thinking, he seized one of the flowers nearest him. It was a simple little daisy. It told him all about itself in a moment—more than a botanist could tell in many lectures. It told the myth about its birth; it told about the power of the sun, which made it spread out its delicate petals, causing them to yield their fragrance. This set him thinking of life's struggles, which in the same way awaken feelings in our breasts. Air and Light were the flower's suitors, but Light was the favored one. The flower bent itself toward the Light, and when the Light disappeared, it rolled up its delicate leaves and slept in the Air's embrace.

"It is the light that perfects me!" said the flower.

"But it is the air that you breath!" whispered the voice of the poet.

FORTUNE'S OVERSHOES

BELIEVE IN THE LIGHT

Voices from the crowd answered, "We heard from God's Law that the Messiah lasts forever. How can it be necessary, as you put it, that the Son of Man 'be lifted up'? Who is this 'Son of Man'?"

Jesus said, "For a brief time still, the light is among you. Walk by the light you have so darkness doesn't destroy you. If you walk in darkness, you don't know where you're going. As you have the light, believe in the light. Then the light will be within you, and shining through your lives. You'll be children of light."

JOHN 12:34-36

THE KINGDOM'S PRIDE AND JOY

What grandeur and what beauty in every room! And the little boy saw everything, for the Bronze Boar went step by step through all the splendor in that palace of delight. Each sight was so wonderful it made one forget all the others, and just one picture fixed itself firmly in the boy's mind, and that one chiefly because of the joyful, happy children that were in it. The little boy had once nodded to them by daylight.

Many people pass quickly by this picture; and yet it has in it much poetry. Jesus is seen descending into the Underworld; but it is not tortured souls we see about him. The heathen are there. The Florentine, Angelo Bronzino, painted the picture. Particularly wonderful is the expression of the children in their certainty that they will go to heaven. Two little ones already embrace each other; one child stretches his hand to another below him and points to himself as if saying: "I am going to heaven!" All the older persons stand uncertain, hoping, or bow themselves humbly before the Saviour in prayer.

At that picture the boy looked longer than at any other. The Bronze Boar rested quietly before it. A soft sigh was heard. Did it come from the picture or from the Bronze Boar's breast? The boy lifted his hand toward the smiling children; then the animal hurried away with him out through the open vestibule.

THE BRONZE BOAR

Illuminated by The Message

THE KINGDOM'S PRIDE AND JOY

People brought babies to Jesus, hoping he might touch them. When the disciples saw it, they shooed them off. Jesus called them back. "Let these children alone. Don't get between them and me. These children are the kingdom's pride and joy. Mark this: Unless you accept God's kingdom in the simplicity of a child, you'll never get in."

LUKE 18:15-17

LET RIGHTEOUSNESS BURST INTO BLOSSOM

He seized the vines and roots and clambered up the wet stones, where the water snakes wriggled and the toads seemed to bark at him. But he reached the top before the sun had set entirely. Seen from that height, oh, what splendor met his gaze! The sea, the vast, wonderful sea, stretched before him, its long waves tumbling against the shore. The sun stood like a great shining altar far away where sea and sky met. Everything melted together in a bright glow of color; the forest sang, and the ocean sang, and he sang with them. All nature was a great holy temple, in which the trees and the swaying clouds were the pillars, flowers and grass a woven tapestry of velvet, and the sky itself the great dome. Far on high the red colors vanished as the sun went down, but millions of stars gleamed out like millions of diamond lamps, and the king's son stretched his arms toward the sky, toward the sea and the forest—and at that moment, from the right, came the poor boy with the wooden shoes and the short sleeves. He had reached the same place by his road. They ran to meet each other, and held each other's hands in the great temple of nature and poetry. And over them sounded the invisible holy bell. Glorious spirits swayed about it, singing a joyous Hallelujah!

THE BELL

Illuminated by The Message

LET RIGHTEOUSNESS BURST INTO BLOSSOM

Give the gift of wise rule to the king, O God,
*   the gift of just rule to the crown prince.*
May he judge your people rightly,
*   be honorable to your meek and lowly.*
Let the mountains give exuberant witness;
*   shape the hills with the contours of right living.*
Please stand up for the poor,
*   help the children of the needy,*
*   come down hard on the cruel tyrants.*
Outlast the sun, outlive the moon—
*   age after age after age.*
Be rainfall on cut grass,
*   earth-refreshing rain showers.*
Let righteousness burst into blossom
*   and peace abound until the moon fades to nothing.*
Rule from sea to sea,
*   from the River to the Rim.*

PSALM 72:1-8

SCRIPTURE INDEX

Acts
- 3:1-11 83

Colossians
- 1:3-8 81

1 Corinthians
- 15:35-41 45

2 Corinthians
- 1:8-11 103
- 7:10-13 33
- 12:7-10 19

Deuteronomy
- 17:18-20 51

Ecclesiastes
- 3:1-8 49
- 9:7-10 107

Ephesians
- 5:21-31 95

Exodus
- 1:8-14 23

Ezekiel
- 36:24-28 105
- 37:2-10 85

Genesis
- 11:1-9 69
- 12:1-8 39

Habakkuk
- 2:5-8 35

Isaiah
- 2:11-18 79

James
- 3:13-18 59

Job
- 8:1-7 47
- 30:9-19 29

John
- 9:31-41 57
- 12:34-36 109

Jonah
- 2:5-10 21

Luke
- 10:33-35 15
- 11:2-9 73
- 12:42-48 17
- 18:15-17 111

Matthew
- 7:15-20 61
- 12:31-37 91
- 12:43-45 65
- 18:1-5 75
- 24:23-28 89

1 Peter
- 3:8-16 31

Proverbs
- 5:15-19 101
- 9:7-12 93
- 14:5-13 53
- 26:1-10 55

Psalm
- 7:1-8 27
- 72:1-8 113
- 84:1-4 87
- 89:25-29 41
- 91:2-12 67
- 104:24-31 63
- 112 71
- 141:1-9 99
- 145:1-7 25
- 149 43

SCRIPTURE INDEX

1 Samuel
   2:2-5 97

Song of Songs
   1:2-4 37

1 Timothy
   1:3-11 77

Mary K. Doyle is a former feature writer for the *Chicago Tribune*, book author, blogger (Doyle's Delights and Midwest Mary), and trade representative for ACTA Publications. She writes and speaks on the topics of caregiving (especially to loved ones with Alzheimer's), aging faithfully, Marian devotion, Saint Mother Theodore Guerin, mentoring, and the joys and challenges of everyday life. She is the devoted wife of magician Marshall Brodien, a mother and grandmother, and a member of an extensive family and circle of friends. One of her favorite hobbies is hand quilting. She has a Master's degree in Pastoral Theology from St. Mary-of-the-Woods College in Indiana, founded by Saint Mother Theodore Guerin. Her many books include *Navigating Alzheimer's*, *The Rosary Prayer-by-Prayer*, *Grieving with Mary*, and *Young in the Spirit*.

LITERARY PORTALS TO PRAYER™

LOUISA MAY ALCOTT

JANE AUSTEN

CHARLES DICKENS

ELIZABETH GASKELL

HERMAN MELVILLE

WILLIAM SHAKESPEARE

Enhanced-size edition available for each title.

800-397-2282 • ACTAPUBLICATIONS.COM